HUE COLORING

50 Beautiful Horses Designs
An Adult Coloring Book

ISBN-13: 978-1523605224
ISBN-10: 1523605227
Copyright © 2015 Hue Coloring

IN THIS COLORING BOOK...

Immerse yourself in a stress relieving activity of coloring 50 exquisitely hand-drawn illustrations of horses. Forget about your troubles and find many hours of mental relaxation, enjoyment and creativity by coloring these magical images. Each coloring page is designed with beautiful patterns that appeal to adult eyes.

TIPS TO A RELAXING COLORING

Find a quiet space. It's easier to focus on what you are doing when there are no distractions.

Organize your materials. Lay out your coloring book and crayons, pens, or pencils.

Set the mood. Turn on some tranquil music, diffuse lavender or another relaxing oil, and make sure you have your preferred drink at hand.

Select your picture. Which image speaks to you today? That's the one you should color. Choose your pallette. Select the colors you will be using for your image.

Begin coloring. This is the fun part. Don't worry about getting evrything perfect just start. If you feel you don't want to do it anymore, just stop!

SHOWS US YOUR CREATION!

We'd love to hear from you, show us what you created.
Facebook:www.facebook.com/huecoloring
Pinterest:www.pinterest.com/huecoloring

Please be sure to subscribe to our newsletter by visiting: huecoloring.com We'll show you our latest coloring projects as well as giving you information of the best deals.